Up Close and Personal

Papal Audience and Blessing (1985)

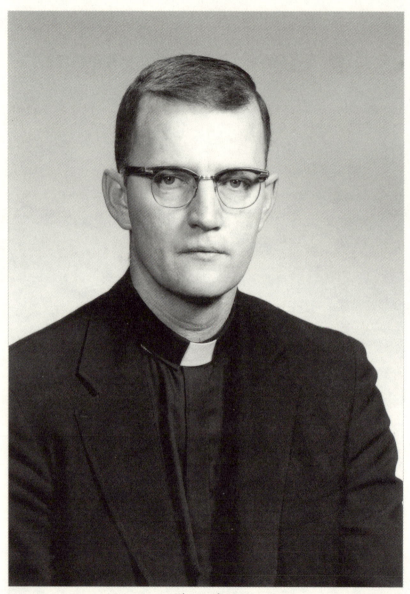

The Author

Up Close and Personal

A Sailor Swims the English Channel

by Robert J. Manning
with Mary I. Manning

Edited by Neal Burdick

Artwork by Charlene Meeker

Bloated Toe Publishing
Peru, New York 12972

Library of Congress Control Number: 2014938046

ISBN 13: 978-1-939216-33-5   ISBN 10: 1-939216-33-8

Copies of this book may be purchased from the author:
Robert Manning
196 E. Hatfield Street
Massena, NY 13662

Front cover designed and created by
Jill C. Jones of Bloated Toe Enterprises
www.bloatedtoe.com   Email sales@bloatedtoe.com

Front cover: the author, Robert Manning, a few days after The Swim
(which accounts for the smile)

Back Cover: Mary and Robert Manning

Printed and bound by
Versa Press, Inc., 1465 Spring Bay Road, East Peoria, IL 61611-9788

Manufactured in the United States of America

*Dedicated to the
memory of my parents,
Rosalie and John,
who gave me life,
and then made it better*

CONTENTS

The author leading a Holy Land tour (1983)

PREFACE

If the earth were a cake, the English Channel and Mount Everest would be super icing. Swimming across one and climbing the other opens one's life to the possibilities of hypothermia and exhaustion. Two frequent and haunting questions are: Why swim across the English Channel? Why climb Mount Everest?

I have answered the first question for myself. I hope that this book helps you answer the same question. A close and personal encounter with the English Channel has earned me unparalleled satisfaction. In the words of the modern man or woman, it is a "super high." Challenging the English Channel is a breathtaking (pardon the pun) experience.

In order to complete a swim across the English Channel, mind, body, and spirit must be right. Unlike many wonderful English Channel swimmers, I have included accounts of my three incomplete swims. I do not consider these swims failures. They were invaluable parts of my training.

I have used my wits and my pen to help you understand and feel what happened. I sincerely hope that my experience with the English Channel will also be enjoyable for you.

1.

Humble Beginnings

About the time I was eight years old, I learned to read. I liked to read the newspaper and look at the pictures. Whenever I came across an article about someone celebrating their 100th birthday, I took the newspaper, ran and showed it to my mother. I thought that living to be 100 years old was so wonderful.

At the same age, I would read about a man or woman who swam across the English Channel. I was so awe-struck by this feat. Sometimes a picture would depict a swimmer with an ecstatic smile, covered with grease, looking like a creature coming out of a canal in a science-fiction movie. To me, they looked great. I was so enthralled with their feat....

I didn't run to my mother with stories about English Channel swimmers. I kept the admiration and wonder to myself.

Thus were "English Channel seeds" sown in my mind and heart. This is the story of those "English Channel seeds" growing, blossoming, and bearing fruit forty-two years later.

I was the oldest of John and Rosalie King Manning's five children. Two sisters, Carole and Barbara, followed me at two-year intervals. Ten years after my birth, my brother Gerald was born. Twenty years after my birth, my youngest sister, Frances was born.

My father, a carpenter, drew unemployment insurance

Two views of my great-grandparents' house in Blarney

most every winter. We did not know that we were poor, but we suspected that we were. My father did not believe in buying anything on the installment plan; he would either pay for an item or do without. That is why we surmised that we were poor. However, we had all the essentials.

Our village of Tupper Lake, New York, had a population of approximately 6,000 residents, then and now. It is located in the beautiful Adirondack Mountains about 35 miles west from Lake Placid. We lived in the heart of the Adirondacks, surrounded by forest. Thus we had plenty of wood for both our kitchen and living room stoves. I was the wood chopper, stacker and all-around wood mover. This helped me develop muscles beginning at age nine. I had plenty of snow-shoveling in the winter months. There was no need to dream of a white Christmas; my siblings and I didn't know any other kind existed.

As well as lakes, including Big Tupper, there were numerous spring-fed ponds throughout the region. Although there was an abundance of fresh water, the closest sea water was the Atlantic Ocean, across the state off the shores of New York City. My first view and experience of the sea water came at age 16, at a Boy Scout Jamboree in Santa Ana, California. The Pacific Ocean's surf and undertow were strong and the Japanese current was cold. For that reason very few could tolerate swimming there, but it provided great experience for a future Channel swimmer.

The author way back when. Torn picture, five kids ... whodunit?

3

My mother in younger years

My parents in front of the homestead

An unexpected surprise added to my experience. On one occasion I was swimming near the shore and spotted what I thought was floating seaweed. Unwittingly I swam into it, trapping the "seaweed" in my right armpit, and immediately felt a sting. I ripped the seaweed off and later found out it was a Portuguese man-o-war.

When I was a young boy, my parents allowed me to go daily to Tupper Lake's beach, and Coney Beach at Little Wolf Pond. I did not know how to swim yet. Eventually, at an older age than the rest of the class, I enrolled in a Red Cross swimming course. The instructor, Brainard Beausoleil, was a kind and patient man, and by the end of that summer, he had me swimming. Thank you, Brainard!

Beginning at age 12, I did get coaching from another source. I joined the Boy Scouts of America, which I enjoyed very much. While I was a sophomore in high school, I was nearing completion of qualifications for Eagle Scout. The last

Boy Scout Jamboree in Santa Ana, California (1953). Author is in the middle row, 2nd from left.

Big Tupper Lake—beautiful for swimming, or just about anything

Tupper Lake, where every Christmas is white

An "elbow shot"—training at Little Wolf Pond near Tupper Lake

two merit badges were swimming and lifesaving. These had the most demanding requirements. Thankfully, I was fortunate to attend Boy Scout Camp for two weeks. At camp was a waterfront director, Mr. Russaw. He was the nicest man you could ever meet, but very strict, just right for Boy Scout Camp.

That summer he coached several of us on swimming strokes and lifesaving techniques. Fun as he was, he did not pass me for the swimming and lifesaving merit badges needed to become an Eagle Scout. He demanded further training and practice before passing me for the needed badges. Thank you, Mr. Russaw! The following year I became an Eagle Scout. Some of the happiest days of my life were spent in Boy Scouts.

We had no swimming pool at Tupper Lake High School. However, other sports helped me keep in shape. Our athletes were usually good enough to win the basketball championship in our league. I was good enough to qualify for Tupper Lake's football and track teams. To stay in good physical condition as a track-team miler, I ran three miles a day. This practice helped me build a good measure of physical endurance.

I graduated from Tupper Lake High School in 1954. Following graduation, I worked as a laborer for the same construction company my father had worked for as a carpenter until I was a sophomore in high school. I wanted to be a doctor.

From the left: the author, his father (John), and the author's brother Jerry

However, a parish priest told me that I seemed to have a calling to the priesthood. Having been brought up in a devout Catholic home, I took him seriously. I prayed to God for guidance. That autumn, I began my studies for the Catholic priesthood at Wadhams Hall College, near Ogdensburg on the St. Lawrence River. While there, I studied liberal arts and especially philosophy, which occupied most of my time. Sports included softball, touch football, and hockey. I played as much hockey as the winter schedule and weather allowed.

I continued my studies for the priesthood at St. Bonaventure University. Scripture and Theology were very demanding. However, there was time to use the university's Olympic-sized (50-meter) swimming pool once a week. This, along with jogging daily and playing basketball, helped me maintain good physical condition.

In 1962, I was ordained to the Catholic priesthood, to minister in the Diocese of Ogdensburg, which included the St. Lawrence Valley and the Adirondack Mountains. Pastoral

The author in second grade

Tupper Lake High School graduation photo (1954)

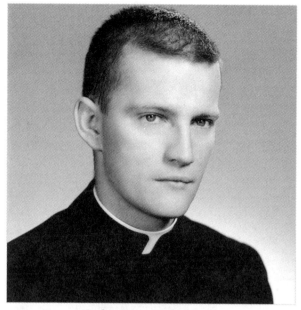

Ordination picture (1962)

After many years as a priest

duties at Notre Dame Church in Ogdensburg left little time for physical exercise. However, a wonderful pastor, Monsignor A. Charbonneau, himself an athlete in his younger days, allowed me to do some hunting.

Following the enjoyable year at Notre Dame, the bishop sent me to Saint Mary's Church at Massena, New York, and

My parents, John and Rosalie, on their 50th wedding anniversary

further assigned me to teach at its Holy Family High School. Thankfully, a kind and wonderful pastor, Monsignor Arthur Leary, who was also Secretary of Education for the Diocese of Ogdensburg, and Father Griffith Billmeyer helped me blend pastoral and teaching duties. I loved working with families at Saint Mary's and with the young people at Holy Family High School. Although physical exercise was limited there, I did manage to play hockey on a General Motors team. Massena was the kind of community where just about everyone loved sports.

The time came for another new assignment. As I was driving to Saint Mary's Parish and High School at Champlain, New York, I cried; I had grown so fond of the people and students at Saint Mary's and Holy Family in Massena, I found it difficult to leave. Soon, though, I found myself attached to the warm French families of Canadian ancestry in Champlain. I felt right at home, being from Tupper Lake village, where 80 percent

The author, with sisters Carole, Frances, and Barbara, brother Jerry, and Dad and Mom in front

were of Canadian background. Most of the families worked and lived on dairy farms. The people of Champlain were a joy to work with because of their love of and respect for priests, along with a great sense of humor.

Although the ministry and teaching were great, my sports and physical activities were once again limited. I much preferred to hunt and fish during my leisure time.

After those wonderful years, the bishop assigned me again to Massena, to St. Joseph's Church and back to Holy Family High School. But as much as I enjoyed teaching and pastoral ministry, I felt a further calling.

My bishop, Stanislaus J. Brzana, having been an Army chaplain during World War II, had a sincere and deep appreciation for men and women in the United States military. He had released several priests for military service. For years, I had had the desire to become a Navy chaplain, so with the encouragement of my very understanding pastor, Father Joseph Dowd, I sent a letter of request to the bishop. He interviewed me and gave me permission to join the United States Navy Reserve. After a year of weekly meetings at the Port of Ogdensburg, plus two weeks' duty at the United States Naval Base in Newport, Rhode Island, I was released from the Diocese of Ogdensburg for active duty in the United States Navy.

2.

To Newport and Okinawa

In Newport, there were several Navy schools geared to indoctrinate professional personnel into the United States Navy. Six of us priests and ministers formed the basic course; senior Navy chaplains and a Marine Corps gunnery sergeant comprised the staff. (The United States Marine Corps is a division of the United States Navy. Marines do not have physicians or chaplains of their own. Physicians or chaplains stationed with the Corps belong to the Navy.)

We clergymen from various parts of the United States enjoyed each other's company as well as the training regimen. We studied the structure and organization of the United States Navy and United States Marine Corps. Our gunnery sergeant taught us to salute properly and to march more or less smartly. We met and interviewed scores of sailors and some Marines. After eight weeks of intense training, we graduated and departed for various duty stations. I was assigned to the Third Marine Division at Okinawa, where I was appointed battalion chaplain to the Second Marine Battalion, Fourth Marine Regiment at a large military base called Hansen. We were already slated for Vietnam. Daily, huge Air Force cargo planes flew over us en-route to Vietnam with supplies.

As a chaplain, I was required to "pack out" for duty

Camp Hansen, Okinawa (1972)

in Vietnam. I trained with the Marine infantry known as the "grunts." I grunted up and down hills, training with Marines half my age. As part of the training, I was proud to complete a fifteen-mile hike with my unit. Most of the young Marines were only about a year older than my high school students, and less than half my age.

Third Marine Division, Okinawa (1973)

The majority of most days were spent counseling. I loved and respected the young Marines. They seemed to sense my care. Consequently I was able to get positive responses most of the time.

As much as I enjoyed serving with the Marines in Okinawa, physical conditioning was limited to hikes, three-mile runs, and military exercises in the field. There was a beach nearby, but the climate and water were too warm for Channel training.

Thankfully, the Vietnam treaty was signed and my battalion never deployed. I led a prayer service thanking God

With school children, Pohang, South Korea (1972)

for peace. Americans need to understand that we chaplains want peace, but it's absent in the world. As chaplains we minister to those Americans who go to war, who are in harm's way. We even hold special services to pray for an end to hostilities. Each and every day I pray for peace.

Okinawa, aside from the World War II invasion, is a peaceful island. The people were very friendly and kind to us Marines and sailors. A group of us went out in our spare time and worked to improve an orphanage. One of our projects was to remove a palm tree from an area needed for expansion. I was born and raised in the conifer forests of the Adirondack Mountains, where both trees and lumberjacks were numerous. More than once I had sawed down trees in and around Tupper Lake. I had no idea how difficult it was to remove a deeply rooted palm tree in the tropics. We had an enjoyable challenge removing those palm trees.

3.

Marine Corps Recruit Depot, Parris Island, South Carolina

My next orders, after a year in Okinawa, were to a Marine Corps Recruit Depot at Parris Island, South Carolina. Parris Island was a real "spit and polish" place. Our uniforms and bearing were subject to daily scrutiny.

I was assigned to the Third Recruit Battalion. Again, most of my time each day was spent in counseling. The young recruits were subject to much stress in training and testing to become full-fledged Marines. They needed understanding, encouragement, and firmness. I tried to blend all three as I guided them morally and religiously to better understand the Marines. I participated in much of their training; a daily three-mile run along with calisthenics kept me in reasonably good shape. The depot swimming pool was restricted, but I did some recreational swims with porpoises at a local beach outside Beaufort, South Carolina.

All in all I found my duties dynamic and enjoyable. Father Tom, the senior Catholic chaplain at the Recruit Depot, had already served several tours with the Marines. His guidance helped me to do much better working with

Terence Cardinal Cooke, Parris Island. Author on left, holding hat (1973).

Father Tom Kelley and the author, Parris Island (1974)

Chaplain Corps Training, senior and junior classes, Newport, Rhode Island. Author is in middle row, second from right.

With my mother, Parris Island (1974)

them. Tom, like me, had taught high school for many years. He could write a letter. Could he really write a letter!

I was further blessed with a superlative commanding officer. General Robert Barrow's kindness, deep appreciation for chaplains, and encouraging words moved me to a quality of service I would not otherwise have achieved. Thank you, General Barrow!

The time came for generals to be promoted. To our surprise, Gen. Barrow was passed over. Tom and I were more than surprised; we were outraged. Tom decided to write a letter to the Secretary of Defense. Around this time, a new Marine Corps Commandant was due to be selected. The Secretary asked all the Marine Corps generals to vote for the general they wanted to be commandant. They voted overwhelmingly for Robert Barrow. As a result, Gen. Barrow went from a two-star to a four-star general, Commandant of the United States Marine Corps, and a member of the Joint Chiefs of Staff. All this added to my enjoyment of Parris Island.

The author at Parris Island

4.

Fleet Religious Support Activity, Norfolk, Virginia

My next assignment took me to Fleet Religious Support Activity, which consisted of chaplains of various denominations, plus a rabbi, who weren't assigned to any particular ship. Our mission was to provide religious and other chaplaincy coverage to Navy personnel on scores of ships in port at Norfolk, Virginia, and at sea. It was an awesome mission.

Our offices were located in a building on the Port of Norfolk shore, adjacent to the U.S. Navy ships in port. In addition to counseling sailors at the office and aboard ship, I scheduled a visit and Mass daily on a ship, a different one each day. On Sundays, I would offer Mass on three different ships.

While in port, I sometimes had time for a noon-hour swim in the pool, conveniently located near our office. This was the beginning of my real swim training. I had been running three miles a day, but with the opportunity to swim came the idea of swimming three miles a day instead. I gradually increased the distance each day.

One wonderful day, I received notice that I would be deploying with five ships to the Mediterranean Sea. Elated as I was, my time at sea would not be compatible with daily swims.

Fleet religious support activity aboard ship (author sporting beard above)

HOLY HELOS — Lt. Bob Manning, right, Catholic chaplain serving a special task group on a European cruise this summer, waits with his Protestant fellow chaplain, Capt. Clarence LeMasters for helicopter service from ship to ship. Navy men refer to the skylifts as "holy helos."
(U.S. Navy photo)

Father Bob Manning Chaplain With Special Navy Task Force Participating in Silver Jubilee of Queen Elizabeth II in England

A Tupper Lake native and former parish priest in the northern tier has a more exotic assignment this month, serving as Catholic chaplain for a special task group of Navy ships participating in the Silver Jubilee Navy Review and 1977 summer midshipmen's cruise, a Navy news release from Portsmouth, England, reports.

"Lt. Bob Manning, son of Mr. and Mrs. John Manning of Tupper Lake, shares responsibility with Protestant chaplain Captain Clarence LeMasters across a seven-ship flotilla which includes the USS California, a cruiser, and USS Billfish, a submarine. Both nuclear-powered ships appeared June 28 in a 150-unit international fleet reviewed by Queen Elizabeth II from her royal yacht, Brittania. The array of dress ships stretched seven miles, across ten rows, off Spithead, near Portsmouth.

"Other ports of call for ships o the task group include Edinburgh Copenhagen and Bremerhaven All seven will return to Norfoll Va. on July 21.

A second major mission of tl six-week cruise is to train 400 s ior and sophomore midshipm from the U.S. Naval Academy a Naval ROTC schools across Am ica.

Lt. Manning, a graduate of Bonaventure and Wadhams F taught at Holy Family School in Massena and at S Mary's in Champlain before joining the Navy five years ago. He also served as parish priest during his teaching days.

His regular assignment is in providing chaplain services to ships in the Norfolk area which do not have a regular chaplain.

About to helicopter to another ship

On one of my deployments, I enjoyed the company of Navy "frog men," or Navy SEALs. They were so helpful to me, bringing me on their boat to different ships for ministry, but neither time nor physical condition allowed me to train under the "frog  men." However, I did swim into Sardinia with them. We had some fun diving for and catching a squid.

Author "high-lining" ship to ship

Evacuees from Beirut (1976)

5.

Naval Regional Medical Center, Charleston, South Carolina

Thanks to our chief of Navy chaplains, we chaplains had a wonderful practice: we could fill out a "dream sheet" of three duty stations to which we would like orders. My first "dream" was London, England; my second was the Naval Regional Medical Center in Charleston, South Carolina; and my third was Morocco.

My second dream was granted. I was pleased because I wanted to minister to the sick.

Before I could make the move, though, in 1964 I underwent hernia surgery in a Canadian hospital. A few days after the surgery, I suffered a pulmonary embolism and nearly died. Pleurisy settled in one lung. After thirty days in the hospital, thanks be to God, I recovered without permanent damage. The experience was the best preparation I could have had to understand and minister to ill people.

The Naval hospital at Charleston was truly a dream come true. Charleston, after San Diego, was the most preferred retirement location for both sailors and Marines. For that reason, many hospital patients and their families were older than active-duty military personnel.

I was fortunate to have as my senior chaplain Commander Hoyt Swann, a Southern Baptist minister. He was all-around superlative, with a great sense of humor. Of all the great chaplains with whom I have worked, Hoyt was one of the finest.

Hoyt and I ministered to Protestant and Catholic personnel respectively. Our "flock" included scores of retired military in the Charleston area. Besides daily duty at the hospital, we were on call for emergencies. Because my living quarters were only about five miles from the hospital, I could respond to any emergency call within minutes. Given the presence of so many retirees, our duties included conducting frequent funerals.

Fortunately, a few blocks from the hospital, Pepperdine University offered an extension course for a master's degree in Human Relations and Management. Two nights a week, I took

Author, secretary Alice Southern, and chaplain Hoyt Swann at Naval Regional Medical Center, Charleston, South Carolina

four-hour courses. The proximity to the hospital allowed me to be at a patient's bedside within ten minutes in case of need. Evenings, when not in class, I was home doing homework and available for emergency calls.

Another part of the "dream come true" was the Charleston Naval Base swimming pool, located about a quarter mile from the hospital. The pool, not quite Olympic size (50 meters), was 50 yards ... good enough. It was open until till 2000 hours (8 p.m.) daily. My ordinary work day began at 7 a.m. and ended at 4 p.m., so I could begin swimming at about 4:30. I would swim until 7:30. As when in class, if I was needed at the hospital they knew where to reach me. I was just minutes away.

In my spare time, I read books on swimming exercises and strokes, and still wished to swim rather than run three miles a day. I enrolled in American Red Cross life-saving and water safety courses. The instructor, the swimming coach at The Citadel, helped us with our various strokes. Following a few weeks of his coaching, I completed qualifications for life-saving and water-safety instructor. This resulted in improvement of my swimming strokes. I practiced my swimming strokes daily, wore

The Charleston Naval Base swimming pool

paddles on my hands and gained added strength in my arms. I continued working on my goal of swimming three miles a day. After a few months, I found it easier to swim rather than run or even walk that distance. Swimming three hours a day plus 100 push-ups and calisthenics after swimming resulted in a high degree of physical fitness.

At a local bookstore I found several books on swimming. As I studied the strokes and practiced, my swimming improved. I began reading books written by or about distance swimmers. I knew that I was not a fast swimmer, but that I had a high degree of endurance.

Distance swimmers, especially Channel swimmers, fascinated me. I began imitating their eating habits. After each hour, I would drink a cup of Ensure, a health drink. That cup gave me the nourishment I needed. As I swam more and read more, I came to the conclusion that I too could swim the Channel.

In one of the popular magazines, perhaps *Time* or *Sports Illustrated*, I came across a feature article about James Edward "Doc" Counsilman, a 58-year-old swimming coach at Indiana University and United States Olympic Coach. He had swum across the Channel. I was impressed and inspired and, as luck would have it, one of Doc's top swimmers at Indiana University was coaching swimmers in Charleston. I immediately contacted Gary Conelly and asked him to help me train. He agreed to help me for a very modest fee.

Gary was the alternate on the Olympic swimming team with Mark Spitz. Unfortunately, Doc Counsilman was not coaching the year those two went to the Olympics. Gary could have and should have won a Gold Medal for a relay swim. Anyway, Gary gave me swimming pointers and inspiration that helped me cross the English Channel. Thank you, Gary!

Being a Red Cross water safety instructor, I offered certified swimming instructions to a class of sailors, mostly nurses. It gave me great satisfaction that they all learned how to swim. I conducted another class at a Charleston municipal pool

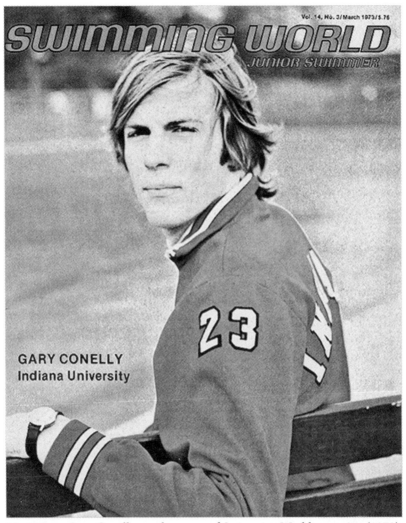

Vol. 14, No. 3/March 1973/$.75

SWIMMING WORLD

JUNIOR SWIMMER

GARY CONELLY
Indiana University

My trainer, Gary Conelly, on the cover of *Swimming World* magazine (1973). In 1972, he was an alternate on the US Olympic swim team led by Mark Spitz.

not far from my residence. I also had the opportunity to work for a short time as a lifeguard there.

I trained on my own for a few months. Gary put me in contact with a retired policeman in Texas who was an English Channel swimmer. The Texan, for a considerable amount of money, agreed to coach me by letter and later on site in Dover, England. Our contact was by telephone only. I was used to taking a day off from training each week; he insisted that I train every day. About the only other coaching was to take cold, not hot showers. I trained every day.

And then a wonderful thing happened: I received orders to the United States Naval Activity in London, England. I was especially joyful to get this notice, because duty in London would have me closer to Dover and the Channel.

6.

On Leave at Tupper Lake

Following my two years of duty at the Medical Center in Charleston, South Carolina, and prior to my two years at the Naval Activity in London, I was given thirty days' leave. I spent my leave time where I always did: at home in Tupper Lake, New York. I enjoyed the family company along with my mother's home cooking, and was delighted to worship again at St. Alphonsus Church. Monsignor Edmund Dumas and Father Donald Manfred were always cordial.

I decided to do what the apostles did: I went fishing. My father, a licensed Adirondack guide, brought me trout fishing and I enjoyed catching a few speckled trout.

I was glad to be home and see so many relatives and friends in my hometown. Tupper Lake is a friendly village. Campers, golfers, fishermen, and other tourists increase the summer population. First-class ski slopes attract winter tourists. Tupper's friendly people attract me all the time.

Up to this time, I had pretty much kept my Channel aspirations to myself. I revealed my plans to my mother, who was immediately supportive, and to my father, who was skeptical, but also supportive. He was so supportive that he rowed his guideboat, escorting me while I trained on Little Wolf Pond, about 60 degrees Fahrenheit in early June.

Another "elbow shot"—me training at Little Wolf Pond

I soon realized that swimming parallel to the shore gave me the training I needed. My father would park along the shore and wait for me to complete four or more hours of swimming each day. He was content to sit in his vehicle and read a book, patiently waiting for me to finish. His support was of immeasurable value.

My mother was always my best cheerleader. She was captain of my cheerleading squad, which also included my sisters Carole, Barbara, and Frances, and my brother Gerald, who paddled his canoe escorting me as I swam some 18 miles, the length of Big Tupper Lake.

I continued to swim every morning in cool 60-degree water, while my father stood by. Every hour I would drink a

Just finished swimming the length of Tupper Lake

cup of Ensure; at lunchtime, I would load up on bananas. Any marathon athlete needs to keep his or her potassium level up, and bananas fill that bill.

My Texan trainer insisted I swim every day without fail. My family gave me love and support and their prayers. My bishop, the Most Reverend Stanislaus Brzana, was also very encouraging and supportive.

My last training day included an eight-hour swim at Little Wolf Pond. After a bus ride to New York City, I boarded a Pan American flight to London, England.

7.

United States Naval Activity, London, England

United States Navy Activity was located on Green Street across from the U.S. Embassy, a few blocks from Hyde Park. My quarters were the London Elizabeth hotel, on the edge of the park. As luck would have it, I was within walking distance (about one and half miles) from the Naval Activity. I would sometimes walk to work, but more often, in the interest of time, I would take the Underground (subway). Further, one of the most popular swimming facilities was located in the park between my quarters and the Naval Activity. Hyde Park was designed to accommodate walkers, joggers, dog walkers, picnickers, and swimmers. The water canals and lido (a British term for a public outdoor swimming pool and surrounding facilities) were designed in the form of a serpent, and named The Serpentine accordingly. Each day the lido accommodated hundreds of Londoners from daylight to dusk. The Serpentine also accommodated scores and scores of Canada geese, swans, and a variety of waterfowl.

During most of the daytime hours, a lifeguard was on duty. The swimming crew at the lido, i.e., my Texan trainer, had alerted me to The Serpentine. I lost no time in locating and

Author with two groups from the Serpentine lido in London

orienting to such a wonderful and suitable training facility and in meeting a most congenial Scottish superintendent, Jacques Pederson. He couldn't have been more helpful in acquainting me with the wonderful features of the lido.

I asked Jacques about Rosemary Franklin-George. My Texas trainer had given me her name and told me that she had swum the Channel. Jacques told me that she was a lifeguard. She was "very blonde," Jacques had said. She would be coming along each day about 3 p.m.

A day or two later, I was there when she came to work. I introduced myself, told her of my intentions of swimming the Channel, and asked her help. In her quiet way, she agreed to assist me.

A few days went by and I was exhausted from swimming every day, as the Texan had directed. I had been over-training. The Texan was training six of us and was going to be with us in Dover Harbor for a few days.

Rosemary suggested beginning in Dover by swimming in the harbor. So on my next day off I went to London Bridge train station and bought a round-trip ticket to Dover. I boarded the train and after a ride through beautiful countryside, I arrived at my destination.

This was a true adventure for me—my first trip to Dover, England, and no one to talk to. I looked around and followed the seashore until I spotted what appeared to be a beach. There was no one there except me. The air was cold and the water was no warmer than 60 degrees Fahrenheit. I took off my sweat suit and sneakers, laid them on the stones, and proceeded to enter the sea as I always entered a river: I waded in, washing water over my body until I became accustomed to the temperature.

I swam back and forth for three hours. I then walked toward Saint Paul's Church and paid my respects to the pastor. He graciously agreed to allow me to stay at the rectory during my training days.

I boarded the train and returned to London. There I

Rosemary Franklin-George, (unknown), author, swim star Jon Erikson

continued to provide counseling to Navy personnel. Red Cross calls came in regularly, and I often would be called upon to inform someone of the serious illness or death of a family member. This was my most unpleasant task. Often, we would have difficulty locating a sailor's residence in civilian quarters in the city, and then would learn that the sailor was traveling. I also gave religious instruction and assisted the Alcoholics Anonymous group.

On Sundays, I boarded the subway and rode for an hour to our chapel on the outskirts of the city. Each Sunday, we had both Catholic and Protestant services at the chapel. There was a concentration of sailors and their families in the vicinity of the chapel.

London is a fabulous city. Wait and Hollywood comes to you. I loved reading *The London Times*, where I once noted that Dolly Parton was scheduled to sing in one of London's downtown theaters. I called and got tickets for myself and my successful Channel-swimming friend, Robert Lyle.

There are thousands of Americans living throughout London. It seemed like they all bought tickets to Dolly's concert. Robert and I took our aisle seats in the center of the auditorium, but I had spotted empty seats on a side aisle, closer to the stage. Robert and I moved and took them.

Finally, the great time came and Dolly entered the theater, not on the stage, but down the aisle where we had been sitting. To my surprise and dismay, she kissed and hugged the lucky fellow who had taken our old seats. So I can now say that I was almost kissed by Dolly Parton, who gave a wonderful performance that night. I can also say that although I was a priestly celibate, I was neither deaf nor blind.

To swim the Channel, you have to mean it. You have to train each morning. I rose in the dark, dressed, ate cereal, and drank some coffee. Dressed in my black clerical clothing, I would walk to the lido in Hyde Park. Some members of the

Lido Club, to which I belonged, went there for early-morning swims. The air was as cold as the water. We shared the lido with dozens of Canada geese and other waterfowl that left generous deposits of droppings on the concrete lido landing. The workers could not keep up as they swept and shoveled droppings into the water. We swimmers had to go with the flow. Each morning, I was able to get in a mile or two of swimming, then continue walking another mile to the office.

To swim the Channel, you have to mean it.

8.

The Channel

We Americans know the English Channel as a stretch of water bordered on the northwest by England and on the southeast by France. It extends from the Atlantic Ocean in the southwest to the North Atlantic in the northeast. The British shoreline is capped by white limestone cliffs, well known as the White Cliffs of Dover. On a clear day, one can stand on the English shore, look across the Channel, and see equally beautiful white cliffs capping the French shoreline.

The English graciously recognize that the Channel is bordered by France as well as England, and thus refer to the body of water as the Channel. We in the United States use the term "English Channel"... a misnomer. The French refer to the Channel as La Manche—"the sleeve"—because of its sleeve-like shape.

The narrowest part of the Channel extends from Saint Margaret's Beach, England, to Cape Gris Nez, France—a distance of seventeen miles. We won't say as the crow flies, because crows don't fly there. We might say as the seagull flies.

As far as the average swimmer is concerned, the Channel water is cold, and it stays too cold for many excellent swimmers. By July and August the water warms up from about 52 to 62 degrees Fahrenheit. However, some swimmers are able to complete a swim as early as June and as late as September. Off Cape Gris Nez, the temperature runs about two degrees warmer than in the rest of the Channel, just right for jellyfish. A bite from a jellyfish can prevent a swimmer from going on. On occasion, a swimmer has been stung by a jellyfish and felt as  though he or she had flu-like symptoms, but recovered and was able to complete the swim. Generally, though, jellyfish can be a concern.

Other sea critters are not. One non-worry is sharks. Basking sharks are so named because they surface and bask in the sun, never bothering a swimmer. I swam in the Channel for about three years and never once saw a shark. I never even heard of anyone seeing a basking shark. That was all right with me!

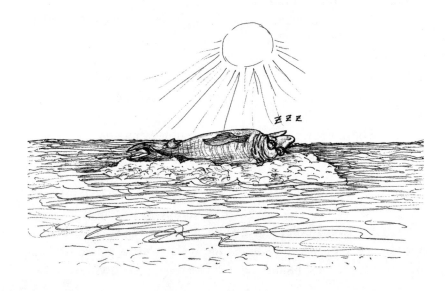

Sharks are not to be feared; you leave them alone and they will leave you alone.

Tides, however, are a concern. Neap tides are the lower tides. Spring tides are characterized by faster-moving, deeper water. Swimming the Channel is possible on the neap tides when the tidal current is weaker. The greater range of the spring tides occur when the moon and sun are aligned and pulling together, as at new and full moon. The lesser neap tides occur when the moon is halfway between new and full. This is when a swimmer has the best chance to start a Channel attempt. The fishermen escorts are experts on the Channel tides and weather, and this is what they advise.

I have noted that the shortest distance across the Channel is seventeen miles. However, no swimmer can swim seventeen miles straight across the tides because they change, causing the swimmer to swim a big "s"—more than seventeen miles. The

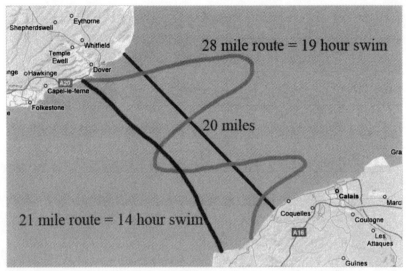

28 mile route = 19 hour swim

20 miles

21 mile route = 14 hour swim

Americans refer to it as the English Channel. The British, acknowledging France on the opposite shore, call it simply the Channel. The French refer to it as La Manche—the sleeve—because of its sleeve-like shape. Though the narrowest width is 17 miles, tides force swimmers to follow an "S" pattern.

faster the swimmer, the smaller the "s." Every Channel swimmer wants to swim across its cold waters as quickly as possible. (I was a slow swimmer.)

The Channel is one of the busiest shipping lanes in the world. Each day ships from all over the world pass through. Although 50-foot fishing boats escorting a swimmer have the right-of-way, a large vessel cannot always change course. Other ships are passing through at the same time. A larger ship unable to change course may cause termination of a swim. Thankfully this was never a problem on any of my swims. Many ships did cross my path. Their churning propellers brought cold water up from the bottom. After a ship passed, I would swim through a quarter to half mile of colder water. I was happy to get back into relatively warmer 62-degree water.

9.

Swim One, July 26, 1982

I went on a seven-day leave of absence from the United States Naval Activity, boarded a train in London, and traveled to Dover. At Dover, I checked in with the pastor at Saint Paul's. Both he and the housekeeper were very gracious. I told them that I would provide my own meals.

Three other American trainees and our Texan trainer were scheduled to arrive in Dover the next day. The trainer had directed me to get "Channel grease" from the chemist, as the British call a drug store. I really didn't know the contents of Channel grease. The young worker at the chemist did not know either. After some hassle, the chemist sold me a five-pound mixture of lanoline and Vaseline.

I returned to the rectory and added the Channel grease to my supplies in a cardboard box: two large bath towels, five gallons of potable water, and several packages of Compline, a British health drink similar to Ensure. Compline powder came in vanilla, strawberry, and chocolate. I was satisfied with just the vanilla and strawberry. I also had a container of "fairy liquid soap" needed to remove the "grease" after the swim. Included in my supplies were several mini-Mars bars, along with a half dozen bananas. My breakfast consisted of a bowl of cold cereal and a couple of bananas. Lunch was two bananas and a chocolate

Staff Photo by Bill Jordan

In The Swim

Lt. Cmdr. Robert J. Manning, chaplain at the Naval Regional Medical Center, prepares for his attempt to swim the English Channel, a feat he plans to try this summer.

Getting ready for Swim One

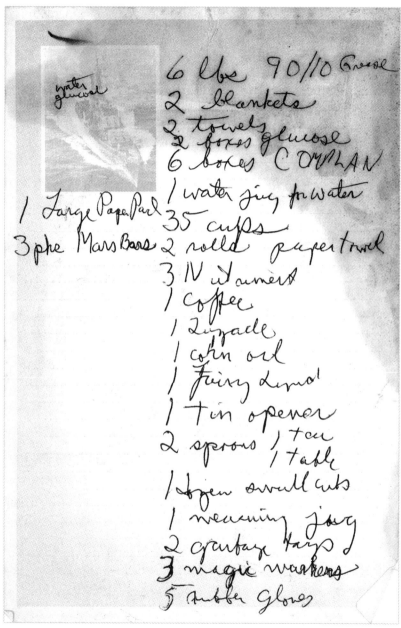

Supply list, Swim One

bar washed down with a cup of vanilla Compline.

After lunch I walked to the harbor and swam for three hours, then returned to the rectory for a leisure period. After dinner, I settled down for a good night's sleep. The following morning, after cold cereal and coffee, I walked down to the harbor. On the beach were myself, my trainer, and the three other trainees.

We got right down to business and swam three hours in the harbor. Lisa Kelsey was an Olympian who, along with other American athletes, was not allowed to participate in the Olympics that year, a decision of President Jimmy Carter. She tolerated the cold and did well that morning. One trainee could not tolerate the cold water, but the other fellow and I did all right. It was our first day of training.

That afternoon, our trainer arranged an appointment with Audrey Scott, secretary of the Channel Swimming Association.

Trainers at Dover, including Olympian Lisa Kelsey. Author is on far right.

We taxied over to the fishing harbor in Folkestone, England. Audrey was very gracious and helpful as we registered for our swims, paying the usual fee. We also needed to register the fishing-boat escort, its captain, and the day of the swim. It was Wednesday; I registered to swim on Sunday morning, providing the weather allowed.

We returned to Dover that evening. I joined the group for dinner at their hotel and enjoyed eating and visiting with the young athletes. At age 48, I could refer to them, half my age, as young.

The next day, we continued training in the harbor. Lisa swam much faster than any of us. I would plod along at my usual pace. We trained Wednesday, Thursday, and Friday. My trainer told me that I was slated to swim Sunday morning from St. Margaret's Beach, England, to Cape Gris Nez, France. Saturday evening, I offered Mass at Saint Paul's Catholic Church. (Along

Approaching the boat for a feed

with our Jewish brethren, Catholics recognize the Sabbath on Saturday.)

Early Sunday morning, following breakfast of cold cereal, banana, and coffee, I took my cardboard box of supplies and set out for Folkestone Harbor. My trainer accompanied me. At Folkestone, we boarded a 50-foot fishing boat. On board, besides myself, were the captain, his mate, the Channel Swim Association observer, and my trainer, who helped me by putting the five pounds of Channel grease all over my body. No grease was below my elbows, where it would get on my goggles and break the seal. All that I had on were a swim cap, goggles, swim trunks, and five pounds of Channel grease.

When we got to Saint Margaret's Beach, the boat stopped and idled about 50 yards off shore. I went down the ladder and into the dingy. The mate brought me to shore, where I walked into the water and began swimming out to the starboard side of the boat. About 10 feet from the boat, I continued swimming toward the boat as it headed for Cape Gris Nez, France. My stroke was the most common one used to swim the Channel, the

The author swimming at Dover

overhand crawl, sometimes referred to as the Australian crawl.

The wind came up and "white horses" appeared. We Americans refer to the white water on tops of waves as "whitecaps."

The optimum weather forecast for a swimmer is "no wind." This was not the case.

After one hour, my trainer bent over the side with a cup of Compline. I continued to swim after taking less than a minute to drink it. As I swam, the wind increased and the waves became higher.

I spotted a tanker passing us. No problem; it changed course to avoid us. However, the tanker's huge propeller brought colder water to the surface. About 30 minutes later, I reached the large area of cold water, which lasted for about another 30 minutes. Then the regular water temperature of 60 degrees Fahrenheit returned.

One hour from my last feeding, my trainer gave me another cup of Compline, this time heated with a little tea in it. He told me I was not making headway because of the increasing wind. He suggested I terminate the swim. I told him that I would think about it, and continued swimming.

The "white horses" increased. It was true; I didn't seem to be making any headway. After another three hours, I decided to come out of the water. The other trainee had also terminated his swim. The trainer, as well as the fishermen, got their full fee whether or not I was successful.

Without much conversation, we returned to Folkestone, where I took a taxi back to Saint Paul's Rectory. The very next day I rode a train back to London. I wasn't broken-hearted—just somewhat disappointed, but determined.

10.

Swim Two, August 12, 1982

At The Serpentine, Jacques Peterson, the superintendent, was also disappointed, but sympathetic and supportive of my determination to swim the Channel. Rosemary recommended I join the Serpentine Club and train there. She had trained a number of swimmers, many of them American, to swim the Channel. At that time, she was training Jon Erikson, from Chicago, for the first triple-crossing Channel swim: three back-to-back crossings, with just a short break between. Jon was scheduled to arrive in London soon. Rosemary directed me go to The Serpentine each morning at daylight and after work each day. I did so religiously, pardon the pun.

As the days and weeks went by, my strokes improved, as did my endurance. Rosemary wanted me to complete a twelve-hour swim at Dover Harbor, so in early August 1982 I took a train to Dover. I spent all day swimming in the harbor. Completion of this swim confirmed that I was ready for another attempt at the Channel.

Another set of neap tides was on the charts for early to mid-August. This time, I would attempt to swim from Cape Gris Nez, France, to Saint Margaret's Beach, England. Fair weather was forecast on August 12. The captain, his mate, Rosemary, Mansour Badawi (the Channel Swimming Association observer)

At Folkestone Harbor: (unknown), Mansour Badawi—the Channel Swimming Association Observer, (unknown), (unknown), author

Feeding in calm waters

and I boarded the fishing boat at Folkestone and headed for Cape Gris Nez. Audrey Scott saw us off. It was a sunny day but the wind was increasing. White horses were also increasing rapidly.

At Cape Gris Nez, the French Coast Guard checked my passport. Then I went ashore in the dingy, waded into the water and began my swim. The wind began to pick up; I was bobbing along like a cork in the mounting waves. After two hours I had lunch, one cup of strawberry Compline. The waves were getting so high I was nearly doing somersaults. Thankfully, I was not prone to seasickness.

I was fed again at the beginning of the third hour, with the weather getting worse by the minute. The turbulent waves were blowing me away from the boat. The fishermen were concerned they might lose me.

Finally, Rosemary held up a sign that said You Must Come Out. By this time I expected as much. They hauled me aboard, and so ended my second attempt. We returned to Folkestone and Dover.

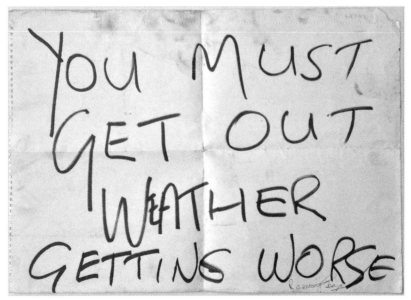

The sign held up by Rosemary to get me out of stormy seas on Swim Two

At the rectory, I took a bath using the fairy liquid soap to get rid of the Channel grease, then returned to London with Rosemary and Mansour. Again I was disappointed, but realized the capriciousness of the Channel water and accepted it. I was still determined to swim all the way across the Channel.

One wonderful and encouraging thing happened prior to Swim Two. A. R. and Sylvia Suritz, a couple in Boca Raton, Florida, read about my ambition and attempts to swim the channel. They and their Jewish friends made donations to help me with expenses. Their generosity paid for half the cost of Swim Two. Although the swim was incomplete, I sent a note of thanks to each donor. Thank you, Mr. And Mrs. Suritz and Friends!

11.

Swim Three, September 13, 1982

You might say that I got my feet wet with the first incomplete swim of six hours. On the second attempt you could say that I got all wet. The Channel, known for its sudden stormy seas, had become very turbulent. I have seen seasoned sailors get sick in those storms. In the face of such conditions, I did not feel too badly over the aborted swim. Having made two attempts at swimming the Channel in just a little over two weeks, I was as determined as ever to swim all the way across.

Rosemary, Mansour, and Jacques continued to encourage me. Rosemary urged me to swim daily in The Serpentine, where a wonderful thing happened: Jon Erikson arrived from the United States. As a teenager, Jon had made a two-way crossing of the Channel. With "all swimmers' muscles," Jon was a superb swimmer. Both he and his father, Ted, had made epic swims of the Great Lakes, especially in the Chicago area.

Rosemary continued to train and advise Jon as he trained at The Serpentine. It was a joy to watch him swim. When a favorable weather report came, Jon asked for my prayers for his success. He and Rosemary drove to Dover, England. About three days later I got a telephone call telling me that Jon had completed the first ever three-way crossing of the Channel. He was a wonderful, inspiring individual.

John Erikson, the first person ever to complete a three-way crossing of the Channel. Overall, he made eleven successful crossings.

I continued my routine of rising in the dark, walking a mile to The Serpentine, swimming for an hour and a half each morning, and then walking another mile to work at the Naval Activity. After a routine workday, I walked back to The Serpentine and swam for several hours before dark. This regimen kept me in superb physical condition.

Another set of neap tides was to occur in September. All we needed was a favorable weather report. On September 9, 1982, high pressure settled over the Channel. There was no wind. We waited.

During this time, I was still an active-duty Navy chaplain stationed at the Naval Activity. On that same day, the Chief of Naval Operations visited us in London, England. At a formal dinner that evening, all of us officers, dressed in our formal attire including cummerbunds, were glad and honored to welcome the CNO. I was delighted to offer grace at the meal. After formalities and travel, I got to bed about 12:30 a.m. This left me tired as I performed my duties the next day. After work hours, a Red

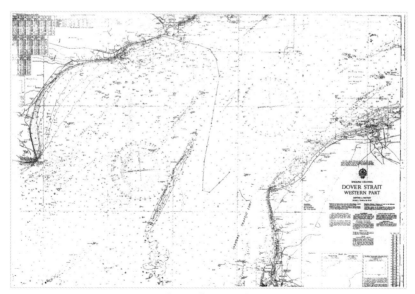

A chart of Swim Three

Approaching the boat to begin Swim Three

Cross call came for a young sailor. It was my job to locate him, inform him of his mother's illness, and see to it that he went on leave for home. By the time I accomplished this it was 1 a.m.

The next morning I showed up for a routine day's work at the Activity. In the afternoon, Rosemary telephoned me that there was a favorable weather report for a swim. She and Mansour would pick me up to travel to Folkestone. My gear and supplies were already gathered in a cardboard box in my quarters.

Later, we drove to Dover, then to the harbor at Folkestone. Before I knew it, they were putting five pounds of Channel grease on me and I began swimming to Cape Gris Nez, France. The sea was calm with no wind. It was ideal for a swim. No bad weather could provide an excuse this time.

However, I had been up late two nights in a row. I am

Mansour, author, Rosemary, her mother Laura

not a night person. The tide had changed and I was being swept parallel with the coast but away from the Cape. I would have had to swim at least seven more hours waiting for the next tide change in order to make it, and I knew I couldn't do that; I was tired when I began to swim.

Why am I doing this? I asked myself.

"I want to come out of the water!" I called to Rosemary.

"Are you sure?" she responded.

"Yes!"

So after thirteen hours of swimming and only about five miles from France, I climbed out, exhausted. We sailed back to Folkestone. I got rid of the fairy liquid soap in a bath. After a few hours of sleep at Saint Paul's Rectory, Rosemary, Mansour and I drove back to London.

The experience left me numb in mind and numb in body. After a few days, reality set in and I realized I had missed my chance. This time I felt extremely disappointed and deeply saddened, after using all that energy and time. I cried. That

Sunday I choked up when I tried to describe my disappointment to my congregation.

The entire experience of Swim Three, though painful, was the most valuable part of my training. Later I shall explain the spiritual significance of this swim.

The reality that hit me was that bad weather had caused me to terminate Swims One and Two. Not so with Swim Three. After thirteen hours and with only about five hours to go, I had given up. When I had come out of the water, I had been tired but not spent. I felt that I could have and should have made it.

I turned to God, to whom I had prayed in my religious tradition, Catholicism. I was used to praying the Mass. As I reflected, it occurred to me that in the Mass we prayed responsorial psalms repetitively, much like our Jewish brethren. Swimming involves much repetition, stroke after stroke. So I decided that from now on I would pray with every stroke.

12.

1983

Even after three unsuccessful swims, I was more determined than ever to swim all the way across the Channel. The Channel swimming season for 1982 was over, at least for me. But "All work and no play can make Jack a dull boy," as the saying goes. Rosemary urged me to stand down from training and simply enjoy swimming. For an attempt at the Channel in 1983, it wouldn't be necessary to resume training until April. Some leisurely and more enjoyable swims would help me maintain good physical condition until then.

A few words about English history and customs may help here. In London, as in any large city, there are homeless people. They do not own a bathtub, let alone a house with running hot water. So that everyone in London might have the opportunity to bathe, the British government constructed swimming pools with baths throughout London. All a homeless person had to do was go to one of the pools or baths and for the equivalent of a quarter, take a nice hot bath. For this reason, there were many swimming pools throughout the city of London.

Enter Bob Manning: once again, my environment was conducive to training. Porschester Bath was only two blocks from my flat on Ossington Street. The pool was not much over twenty-five meters and often crowded, making it a little difficult to establish a lane for distance swimming. However, much of the time that winter I was able to train there.

Better suited for training was Kensington Pool, a larger Olympic-size pool with more available swimming space. Usually a swimming lane was available there, and it was conveniently about a mile and a half walk from my flat. The Portobello Flea Market, on my way to the pool, added interest to the walk on Saturdays.

I was constantly looking for pools suitable for training. I took the Underground to several other pools throughout London, but nearby Kensington and Porschester were convenient for after work, and during the winter months when The Serpentine was less available. Sometimes on a day off, I would take the train to Crystal Palace, the home of the Olympic games; this 50-meter pool was excellent for training and it was just an hour's train ride to the outskirts of London. I even used one pool that fabricated waves; however, most of the time it was crowded with recreational swimmers.

There was another way to train when I couldn't find an available and suitable pool. Walking fast and swinging my arms was conducive to strengthening my swimming muscles. I walked as much as I could to and from pools and also on the London streets. One swimming coach recommended five-mile walks. I enjoyed walking in Hyde Park as well.

One morning, as I was getting ready to leave my London flat to train at a local pool, I received a call from Stella Taylor, a former missionary nun who had conquered the Channel in 1975, swimming from England to France in 18 hours and 15 minutes. At the time, she had given 44 as her age. I had met Stella while I was training for Swim One in Dover, where she was training a swimmer. She cared enough to come by Saint Paul's Rectory to wish me luck before my swim, and returned to cheer me up after my unsuccessful attempt. She was an encouraging cheerleader as well as a genuinely kind friend.

She had called to tell me that she just completed a swim

Stella Taylor, "the Swimming Nun." A highly accomplished marathon swimmer, she twice swam the Channel.

of Loch Ness. I was so delighted for her. She related that she was cold in the famous lake from the beginning of her epic swim.

It is not unheard of that a lady lies about her age. A gentleman friend pointed out that if she had admitted to her actual age of 52, she would likely be the oldest successful female Channel swimmer. So Stella admitted she was 52 and not 44 years old, and was indeed the oldest female to complete a

Channel swim. I was so glad for Stella, who continued to inspire me, "the swimming priest."

I refused to guess at Stella's age. Some of my greatest failures in life have involved trying to guess a nun's age.

Unfortunately, Stella, who worked at the Swimmers Hall of Fame Museum at Fort Lauderdale, Florida, was diagnosed with an inoperable brain tumor in 1991. She passed away in 1993. She was truly a great person as well as a superb swimmer. The news media called her the "swimming nun." Loving God, may she rest in peace. Stella was indeed a beautiful person.

London has many beautiful parks. One such park had several ponds. One pond, Highgate, had a large platform dock where people lifted weights or sun-bathed. I would go to this pond occasionally and swim around and around it. One day as I was swimming, I reached out with a stroke and felt a furry creature. I turned and next to me was swimming a golden Labrador retriever, curious to find out what was swimming in the pond. I exchanged pleasantries with the dog. Thankfully, he was satisfied to see that I was a man swimming. I was glad that

he swam away, for he was a much better swimmer than I was.

On my way to Highgate Pond I used to encounter a fellow who had two beautiful German shepherd dogs. He would bring the dogs up on the bridge. When he gave the signal, both dogs would plunge into the water and swim back to the bridge,

eager to jump again.

I might add here that my swimming workouts included many amusing encounters with sea and other water critters. My encounter with the man-o-war at Huntington Beach, California, was more educational than amusing, since it did prepare me for Channel swimming.

One morning at Little Wolf Pond, I drove an otter out of the water. Had the otter been a female with kits, she would have driven me out of the water. Otherwise it's always fun to see an otter, who are excellent swimmers.

Swimming in cold water, I usually wore a white swimming cap. The cap would rock back and forth as I turned my head while swimming the crawl. Seagulls are used to seeing dead white fish bouncing in the waves, and happy, for dead fish are food for those scavengers. Every once in a while as I was swimming in fresh or sea water, a seagull would approach my head, mistaking it for a fish, then stop and fly away. The first time this happened, I was startled, but after that I was amused. Occasionally a duck or two would drop by and take a good look at me.

I kept training and struggling, and with April, spring arrived. I resumed training at The Serpentine. I swam and swam, wherever and whenever I could. Intent on training in the sea, I took the train to Dover. The hospitality of the kind Irish pastor at Saint Paul's Catholic Church there enabled me to train morning,

Swim, swim, swim at the Serpentine lido

Dover Harbor, where the author trained

The author and Mansour in London (1983)

afternoon, and evening in Dover Harbor. I completed an all-day, 10-hour swim in the harbor, directed by my trainer, Rosemary. I was ready for another attempt on the Channel.

Besides the training swims in Dover Harbor, one more thing was needed ... good weather. The neap tides came and went with the fickle Channel weather. Rosemary did not feel I had a reasonable chance. That year few did! Although I was in superb physical condition, Rosemary did not see a suitable window of good weather.

Rosemary encouraged me to continue training at Twentynine Palms, California, where I had been re-assigned. In October, I returned to the United States, as determined as ever to swim all the way across the Channel.

13.

Marine Corps Air Combat Center, Twentynine Palms, California

There is the desert and there is the deep blue sea. I had experienced the deep blue sea on some 30 ships out of Norfolk, Virginia. Twentynine Palms is desert, part of the Mohave Desert, 2,000 feet above sea level. Within the United States Marine Reservation are the Iron Mountains, a desert area some 50 miles square, available for combat training. Even in the housing areas of Twentynine Palms, the earth would rumble during artillery and am-track firing, as from an earthquake. Sometimes the rumbling was an earthquake!

When I arrived at Twentynine Palms, I saw a beautiful flowering desert with plenty of tumbling tumbleweeds blowing

past me. The ever-so-dry desert had a special charm of its own. Besides daily counseling, my duties involved services at a large chapel, the size of many large churches. I also led regular Bible studies. My responsibilities were

Joshua Tree National Park near 29 Palms

Training at 29 Palms; a rare bathing-suit shot

primarily involved with Catholics, while the Protestant chaplains took care of their communicants at the Protestant chapel.

Thanks to General McIntyre's leadership and support, all went well. Not all was perfect; my personal gear was not sent to Twentynine Palms, but to a female sailor somewhere in South America. This added some stress and expense to my life for several weeks.

But all in all, Twentynine Palms was enjoyable. With my duties as chaplain addressed first and foremost, I began to look for Channel-training assets. Not once did I fail to be available for my duties as a chaplain. Training was fit where it fit. Thankfully, there were two suitable swimming pools at the base—a large 50-meter training pool and an "enlisted" pool. (There was also a smaller but suitable pool for officers.) Both pools were located a couple of hundred yards from the chapel. Because of the cool desert winter, both pools were closed, but the staff at Special Services allowed me to swim an hour or two every day in water that was 50 degrees Fahrenheit. I had the pool all to myself because it was truly cold-water training. The 50-degree water would turn my skin deep red. I swam as much as possible.

By late April and early May, the pool was warmer—warm enough for the troops to resume training. About that time, the officers' pool opened. I would usually get a lane to do laps and train for a couple of hours each day. On a day off, I would swim all day.

The elevation added to the value of my training. Many athletes, especially prize-fighters, would train at high elevation at nearby Bear Mountain. The thinner air demanded more of the human body. This could result in better physical condition. And this was definitely to my advantage.

Palm Springs was about an hour from Twentynine Palms. There I discovered a beautiful municipal pool, an Olympic-sized one at that! I decided to take advantage on my days off. Aside from the lack of cold water, that pool was great for training. A swimming lane was always available for doing laps. I could

Mansour, author's mother, Rosemary

Mansour and the author at the municipal pool, Palm Springs

Mansour, Laura (Rosemary's mother), Rosemary

The chapel at 29 Palms

spend all day training there. In the desert heat, the water would increase to 90 degrees Fahrenheit, while the air temperature was about 100 degrees. From time to time while I trained, I would stand up and expose my body to the air. When we humans are wet and expose our skin to the air, we lose body temperature seven times faster than with dry skin. That is how I managed to stay cool.

Training at Palms Springs was enjoyable overall. One day, late in the afternoon, when most people had left for the day, I looked over at the far end of the pool and there was an attractive lady standing on the diving board. She asked me if I had had a good swim. I said, "Yes" and told her that I was in the military. She asked me what rank I was and I told her I was a lieutenant colonel. She said that I would have to be a general to get with her. I told her, "I will work harder." She continued to dive with graceful skill. I wished her good luck.

My training session would end with calisthenics. Someone, I forget who, had told me Camp Pendleton had a fairly large officers' pool. I found it difficult to find and establish a lane for training. Nevertheless, I was able to get some suitable swimming there a few times.

That winter, my parents were able to come and stay with me for a couple of months. Both my mother and father gave me super company as well as encouragement to swim.

To add to the good company, Rosemary and Mansour came from London to visit for a month. Their company was also encouraging. Thankfully, Rosemary took my parents to some areas of interest, such as Palm Springs, Los Angeles, and Las Vegas.

During my company's stay and after their departure, I continued training at Twentynine Palms and Palm Springs. A Spanish lady gave me some fresh figs, which I enjoyed very much, at hour intervals of training. The days and weeks passed. As the Saint said, "Work as if everything depended on you. Pray as if everything depended on God." I did just that.

Training at 29 Palms

I waited to hear from Rosemary concerning the neap tides. I heard nothing during June and July, and concluded that the right weather did not accompany the tides. Finally, she phoned in mid-August to tell me that a high-pressure system was settling over the Channel.

I was assigned for a two-week leave of absence beginning Monday, August 21, 1984. I made a reservation on Air New Zealand to fly from Los Angeles to London, packed my gear, and drove to Los Angeles airport, all on the same day. Once I was boarded on the aircraft, I enjoyed the company of some tired but interesting Australians who had been flying long hours from their homeland.

14.

The Swim, August 24, 1984

Rosemary and Mansour met me at Heathrow Airport the next morning. They told me the high-pressure air over the Channel stabilized good weather, and that two women had completed their swim. I could hardly wait to get to Dover, but Rosemary wanted me to take two-hour swims Monday, Tuesday, and Wednesday.

On Tuesday, two other swimmers were attempting to cross the Channel. The woman completed her swim, but the man did not. I was ever so eager to get swimming while the weather was so favorable, but Rosemary knew that I still had jet lag and refused to let me swim for two days.

Upon our arrival in Dover, the kind pastor Father David Maher at St. Paul's Catholic Rectory welcomed me. On Tuesday and Wednesday, I took two-hour swims at Dover Harbor. The Channel seas were calm. The weather report was "no wind." Although conditions were ideal for a Channel swim, Rosemary still would not let me make an attempt.

Thursday's weather report was also "no wind," and the forecast for Friday was good. Rosemary telephoned to tell me we would be going to Cape Gris Nez that evening. We had registered my swim with the Channel Swim Association. Rosemary had already contacted Reggie Bricknell and his brother to accompany us with their 50-foot fishing boat, the *Mary Rose*. At the rectory, I packed my gear in my cardboard box. I knew that I should get some rest and sleep, but I was too excited to sleep. I managed to get some rest until supper at 6 p.m. I ate a substantial and reasonable meal. Rosemary had emphasized one dietary restriction: "no milk," my favorite beverage. I had not drunk any milk for a week. I drank water and coffee at mealtimes.

After supper I tried again, but sleep would not come. But I did manage to rest until 8 p.m. At 9 o'clock we left Dover and went to Folkestone. We boarded the *Mary Rose* and at 10 p.m. began our voyage to Cape Gris Nez. Work was still underway on the "Chunnel," the tunnel under the Channel from Folkestone to France, and thanks to the presence of barges and cables, the boat trip from England to France took longer than usual.

I removed my sweatsuit. My swim cap, goggles, and swimsuit remained. The mate and Mansour put Channel grease all over my body, except on my head and below the elbows.

We arrived at Cape Gris Nez at midnight and Reggie stopped about a quarter mile from the beach. The captain presented my passport to French Customs. I climbed down the ladder into the rubber dingy. The mate brought me toward the beach. At the mate's signal, I slid out of the dingy and waded to shore. The mate checked his watch. It was 12:05 a.m. He gave me the signal and I began to swim some one hundred yards toward the bright light on the boat. The swim had begun!

As before, I was swimming the overhand stroke, sometimes known as the Australian crawl. I was about ten feet off the starboard side of the boat. Aside from the bright spotlight to my left, it was pitch black. I could see the occasional glow of a jellyfish.

After two hours, Rosemary came to the rail with a Styrofoam cup. The boat stopped and she handed me a cup of Compline mixed with some hot coffee. I quickly drank the liquid, tossed the cup, and resumed swimming.

Not long after the first feeding, I spotted a huge man-o-war to my close right. I rolled left to avoid contact. Thank God, I did avoid contact! Had I been stung, the swim might have ended.

I continued to swim without incident. Before long I began spotting large tanker ships perhaps a mile ahead of me, safe passing distance. About a half hour later, I would swim into the zone where the tanker had passed and churned colder water up from the bottom.

As much as was going on outside me—calm seas, fair weather, cooperative Channel traffic—powerful forces were at work in me. I was praying with each stroke. "Thank you Jesus." Again and again. "God please help me, I will make it." A prayerful word for every stroke. I was very aware of my connection with God. Once again, my background was to my advantage. Repetition in prayer strengthens our resolve.

What a partner to have: God. I was indeed incomplete without God. My disappointment was so great, especially after my third try, that this time I was so determined to complete the swim that I would have rather died than fail. That was my state of mind. With all this going on inside me, I continued swimming with super resolve, humble enough to realize that I truly needed God's help. So I swam, swam, swam and prayed, prayed, prayed. It doesn't rhyme, but it's powerful.

For the swimmer, environmental variety can be very limited. However, sometime after daylight, I was amused to observe the mate fishing and catching halibut with a hand line. I continued to reach and catch water with each stroke.

"God please help me." It always helps to say please. It did.

My prayers were not without an occasional distraction. I took one stroke and felt a floating garbage bag. Other times, confetti-like paper packing was floating around me. Thankfully there was no photographic opportunity when confetti and garbage decorated me ... a little fun with no problem.

The day passed. Hourly feedings of Compline ...

sometimes a little coffee. Sometimes a small Mars bar. By late afternoon, I was well within view of the English shore. It was fun to see a boatload of tourists come by, waving and cheering. I waved back. The tide and current were carrying me somewhat parallel to shore as the sun set.

At one feeding, Rosemary told me that it would be to my advantage to swim faster for a couple of hours. I couldn't swim any faster. I am what you call a pacer: I maintain a steady pace on a swim, walk, or run, no faster or slower. I just keep going and going. That is what I did.

Just before dark, I could see several tourists on docks along the shoreline. They waved and cheered. It was a very encouraging experience. Thanks again, tourists!

Soon it was pitch black. I continued to swim. I could easily see the lights on the boat. However, the people on the boat had difficulty seeing me, especially as I would sometimes wander away from it. In the pitch dark they would urge me to swim closer.

I really did not feel too tired after swimming 32 miles to travel 17 miles across the Channel. Later, I was to do the mathematics: 49 strokes per minute amounted to 53,655 prayers. I continued to swim, swim, swim … all of a sudden, to my surprise, the boat stopped. This meant that it was close to shore and could not go any closer.

The dingy and mate were lowered into the water. I followed the dingy some 100 yards or so and there was the blessed shore. I walked onto the stony beach. I heard a voice—an angler fishing in the dark. I walked along the shore for a very short way. There, I kissed the ground and thanked God.

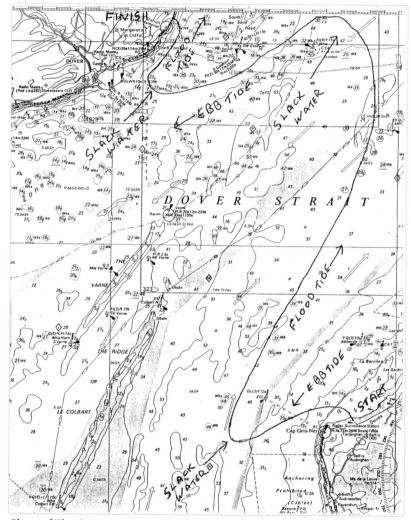

Chart of The Swim, August 24, 1984—17 miles as the crow (or seagull) flies, and 32 miles as the author swam

CHANNEL SWIMMING ASSOCIATION

Founded 1927 Recognised by the A.S.A.

President: Comdr. C. GERALD FORSBERG, O.B.E., R.N. (Rtd.)

Hon. Secretary
Mrs. Audrey Scott
Sunnybank
Alkham Valley Road,
Folkestone, Kent.
CT18 7EH
Tel: 0303 - 89 - 2229

OBSERVER'S REPORT – SOLO SWIM

Name and Nationality of Swimmer: ROBERT J. MANNING; U.S.A.

Name and Nationality of Trainer: ROSEMARY FRANKLIN-GEORGE; BRITISH

Name of boat: HELEN ANN MARIE Skipper: R.W. BRICKELL Crew: RAY BRICKELL

Pilot: R.W. BRICKELL

Any other persons on vessel: MANSOUR BADAWI

Point of start: CAP GRIS NEZ Date: 24 AUG '84 Time: 5.05 A.M.

Grease Amount: 5 lbs. Strokes used: CRAWL

Type: LANOLINE / VASELINE

Time of high water Dover: 9.46 A.M. Height of high water Dover: 6.1 m.

Hour	start	1st	2nd	3rd	4th	5th	6th	7th	8th	9th	10th	11th	12th	13th	14th	15th	16th	17th	18th	19th	20th	21st	22nd
Stroke rate per minute	51	50	50	50	50	50	50	48	49	48	47	47	48	52	51	48	48	48	48				
Wind force and direction	N L	N L	N L	N L	N L	N L	N L	N L	N L	N L	N L	N L	N L	N L	N L	N L	N L	N L	N L				
Sea Temp.	63	63	62	62	62	62	62	62	62	62	62	62	62	62	62	62	62	62	62				

Food taken on swim & duration of stop.	Time	Duration	Food taken on swim & duration of stop.	Time	Duration
Coffee & Complan	7.00AM	30 sec.	Nectar + Mars	3.00PM	3 min.
" "	8.00AM	30 sec.	Choc. Nutrament	4.00PM	2 "
" "	9.00AM	1 min.	Nectar + Mars	5.00PM	3 "
" " + Mars	10.00AM	30 sec.	Coffee + Glucose	6.00PM	4 "
Nectar + Antacid Tablet	11.00AM	1 min.	Coffee + Complan	6.30PM	3 "
Coff. + Complan, Mars	12.00AM	2 min.	Peach Nectar	7.00PM	1 "
Coffee + Date Bar	1.00PM	2 min.	Nutrament	7.45PM	5 "
Coffee + 2 Mars Bars	2.00PM	5 min.	Complan	10.00PM	2 "

Point of finish: Date 24 AUG 84 Time 11.20 PM Total Time 18 hrs. 15 min.

2 Miles East

ST. MARGARETS BAY

I hereby certify that I accompanied ROBERT J. MANNING on date 24 AUG. 84 and that the swim was made in accordance with the rules of the Association.

Signed: M. Badawi

Observer

Please complete Log on reverse side. Date 24 AUG. 84

Record kept by Channel Swimming Association observer

Erratum 1983		**Hrs**	**Mins**
E/F 244	Kevin Murphy (should read).....................	15	29

1984 SOLO SWIMS

England to France

258	Phillip Reed (Wales)............................	14	00
259	James Blears (England).........................	17	10
(i) 260	Alison Streeter (England)........................	10	06
261	Margaret Broenniman (U.S.A.)....................	10	37
262	Maura Fitzpatrick (U.S.A.).......................	11	15
(ii) 263	Michael Read (England).........................	14	05
(iii) 264	Taranath Shenoy 1st leg of 2-way (India)............	10	55
265	Douglas Minde (England)........................	17	14
(iv) 266	Monique Wildschut (Holland)....................	8	19
267	Jordi Martinez (Spain)..........................	10	04
268	Chris Verbrugge (Belgium).......................	13	50
(v) 269	Allan Vandyke (England)........................	13	03

France to England

(vi) 153	Lyndon Dunsbee F/E record (England).............	8	34
154	Michael Read (England)..........................	13	24
155	Kevin Murphy 1st leg of 3-way (England)............	14	58
156	Christopher Stockdale (England)...................	14	50
(vii) 157	Rev. Robert Manning (U.S.A.)....................	18	15

TWO WAY

England/France/England

14	Osama Ahmed Momtaz (Egypt)...................	21	37

RELAY SWIMS

England to France

68	Birmingham University Team (Britain)..............	10	26
69	Dorchester Lifesavers Team (Britain)...............	13	51
70	Howe Bridge Channel Team (Britain)...............	12	16
71	Eltham Training & Swimming Club (Britain).........	12	50

France to England

39	Fraser Court Relay Team (Britain).................	17	27
(viii) 40	B.L.D.S.A. Junior Members (Britain)..............	8	46

(i) Holder of the Sunny Lowry Trophy
(ii) King of the Channel 31 Crossings
(iii) The Van Audenaerde Special Award for Handicapped Swimmers
(iv) Holder of the Sotiraki Trophy and winner of the Rolex Watch

Channel Swimming Association swims for 1984

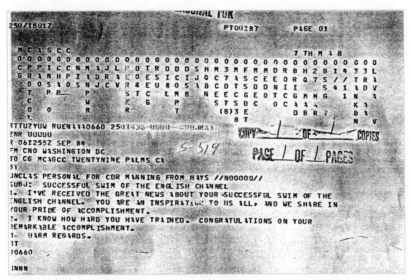

Congratulatory message from Chief of Naval Operations Admiral Ron Hays

Eight years after The Swim, my retirement from the Navy (1992)

Epilogue

The mate helped me to get back into the dingy. We returned to the fishing boat, where they hauled me aboard. I lay back in a corner, talking to Rosemary and Mansour. Rosemary tells me that my first sentence was "Never again." Frankly, I don't remember saying that. I am sure that I had no intentions of making another swim across the Channel.

I was somewhat tired. My throat felt raw from the salt water. I had followed Rosemary's advice to refrain from drinking milk, and for that reason, I did not feel at all nauseous. The salt water would have curdled any milk in my stomach.

After a short boat trip we arrived in Folkestone. The secretary of the Channel Swimming Association, Audrey Scott, and her husband met and congratulated me. Mr. Scott produced a toast. Rosemary and Mansour drove me back to Saint Paul's Rectory in Dover, and Mansour stayed overnight at her mother's residence in Dover.

As I climbed the stairs in the rectory, the kindly Irish pastor met and congratulated me. He also produced a bottle of wine. We had another victory toast. I took a bath and cleansed the Channel grease from my body. Most of it had washed off at sea. I'd lost about five pounds. I slept until about 10 the next morning, when about all I could eat was a soft-boiled egg and a slice of bread. My sore throat made breakfast a little difficult.

It was a beautiful summer day. The high-pressure air mass was still over the Channel. I met a Dutch lady, a super

Channel swimmer, and her husband. She was elated that I'd made the swim.

I returned to the rectory, where I enjoyed the pastor's company and stayed overnight. The next day I offered one of the Sunday Masses, giving thanks out loud to Jesus for my swim. I thanked the pastor for his kind hospitality.

Shortly after, Rosemary and Mansour picked me up at the rectory and we returned to London. I still had a few days' leave. I rested and enjoyed the company of friends at The Serpentine. Jacques Peterson was elated over my swim. He had been such an inspiration. A few members of the press came to The Serpentine, where I enjoyed photographic opportunities. After I returned to the Naval Activity, *Navy Times* personnel took a picture and wrote an article.

After all this, I flew back to Twentynine Palms from Heathrow Airport. There, General William R. McIntyre congratulated me at a public ceremony. I thanked God, the general, and my friends, and continued to enjoy the emotional high predicted by Rosemary.

This account of my living, training, and swimming is as much about prayer and God's blessings as it is about swimming.

Acknowledgments

Thanks to everyone who helped me cross the Channel and produce this book:

Rosemary Franklin-George, for being a friend and trainer, whose encouragement and energy brought sunshine to cloudy days.

Mansour Badawi, a cheerful and cheering friend.

Rosalie and John Manning, for giving me life, then making it better.

Carole, Barbara, Jerry, and Frances, for giving me such good company and enhancing my life.

Brainard Beausoleil, for teaching me how to swim.

Harry Russaw and Gary Conelly, for teaching me how to swim better.

Ted and Jon Erikson, Stella Taylor, Michael Read, and Lisa Kelsey, for their inspiration and friendship.

Gail Deutch, for her inspiration as a swimmer and water safety instructor serving the disadvantaged.

Jacques Peterson, whose words and support helped me swim better.

Audrey Scott, for being so kind and supportive.

Ray Scott, for a timely toast.

Dan McClelland, for his support and published kind words.

The Most Reverend Stanislaus J. Brzana, Bishop of Ogdensburg, for his spiritual leadership, blessing, and encouragement.

Monsignor Edmund Dumas and Father Donald J. Manfred, for their cordial hospitality at Saint Alphonsus Catholic Church and Rectory, Tupper Lake, N.Y.

Father David Maher, for his hospitality and support at Saint Paul's Church and Rectory, Dover, England.

Father Tom Kelley, for his fraternal guidance and advice at Parris Island.

General Robert Barrow, for his superb leadership and guidance.

Admiral and Mrs. Ronald Hays, for superlative leadership and encouragement.

Kaly Sophie White and D. Bow White, for their research contributions.

Emily Hutchinson, for her referrals.

Elaine Dunne-Thayer, for her assistance in research and all-around help at Massena Public Library.

Debbie Fuehring, for her assistance at Massena Public Library.

Michael Griffin, Director of News and Digital Context Services at Clarkson University, for his kind assistance and referrals.

Catherine Sajna at SUNY Potsdam and Clarkson University, for her advice.

"Fonda" at UPS for her informative help.

Tom Stubbs, of Stubbs Printing, for his kind help.

J. David Atwater, for his wonderful Christian inspiration and friendship.

David Tisdale, for being such a valuable friend, ever encouraging and richly helpful.

Neal Burdick, editor at St. Lawrence University, for his editorial skill and gentlemanly, patient assistance in locating a publisher.

The love of my life, my wife, Mary, for among so many other things her patient work, typing at the computer, without whom this book would not have been possible.

Charlene Meeker, my talented friend, whose advice and artwork has so richly enhanced this book.

Special thanks to my publishers, Lawrence Gooley and Jill Jones of Bloated Toe Enterprises, for their expert and congenial assistance. Their expertise and patience compensated for my limitations and resulted in this beautifully published book.

Three-fold thanks to anyone I may have forgotten.